THE BACKOFFICE

BLUEPRINT

FOUNDATIONS EVERY
NONPROFIT LEADER NEEDS

THE BACKOFFICE BLUEPRINT

FOUNDATIONS EVERY NONPROFIT LEADER NEEDS

by

Delton de Armas

and Adam J. Moffitt

ICNU PRESS

Ocala, Florida

TABLE OF CONTENTS

PREFACE

THE BACK OFFICE doesn't change lives. But it can make or break the work that does.

In 2011, I stood in front of a room full of church administrators at a national conference—teaching a workshop on accounting. Not exactly where I pictured my life going. But I was working as the National Relationship Manager for a CPA firm that focused on churches and nonprofits, and I had teamed up with one of the partners to create a course we called *The Accounting Champion*. Fellowship One, a leading church management software company at the time, invited us to present it.

The workshop wrapped up. People filtered out. I gathered my notes—then paused. *This isn't just a presentation… this could actually help people.*

Then, like so many of us do, I saved it to Dropbox and forgot about it.

Years later, after launching Qavah Ministries with my wife, I found myself on the other side of the equation—not the one teaching, but the one searching for answers. The same financial systems I once helped others understand, I now needed.

So I pulled up those old notes. Not to write a book. Just to survive that season.

But as I read through it, piece by piece, I started to realize— the content still worked. Even years later. Even from the other side. What I found wasn't just helpful—it was humbling. I'd written the exact playbook I was now trying to follow. And that's when it hit me: these principles weren't just for churches using a certain software. They applied to any mission-driven organization trying to build something that lasts.

That's how this book was born.

What you're holding comes from years of wins and losses, spreadsheets, and sleepless nights. It's been tested in classrooms and boardrooms, in budget meetings and during *oh-no-it's-audit-season* panic. It's not just about compliance. It's about clarity, sustainability, and integrity.

Because here's the truth: too many churches and nonprofits rely on what's in someone's head instead of what's written down. And when those key people leave—and they always do—the whole system can unravel. I've seen it. I've lived it.

But it doesn't have to be that way.

Whether you're a church accountant stepping into unfamiliar territory, a nonprofit leader without formal financial training, a board member seeking to strengthen oversight, or a volunteer treasurer wondering where to start—this book is for you. It bridges the gap between complex accounting principles and practical ministry needs, providing a guide that anyone can follow.

This isn't just a boring manual. It's a practical blueprint. One you can adapt to fit your team, your vision, and your calling. If it helps you build a back office that actually supports your frontline work—then it's done what it's supposed to do.

And if, somewhere along the way, God works in you, through you, or even in spite of you… well, that wouldn't surprise me one bit.

Here's to building something beautiful—especially the parts no one sees.

A Word About Voice and Collaboration

Though most of this book is written in the first person for ease and clarity, *The Backoffice Blueprint* is very much a collaborative work. I (Delton) started laying the foundation years ago, drawing from both my failures and my wins. Adam came alongside this vision, bringing his own experience and insights to strengthen and sharpen every chapter.

Rather than interrupting the flow with "we" or footnotes about who wrote what, we've chosen to keep the tone conversational and consistent. When you read "I," think of it as the lived experience and voice of the practitioner—and know that the ideas and guidance offered here reflect the combined wisdom and heart of both of us.

Our goal is to give you a framework that works, whether you're starting from scratch or shoring up a back office that already exists. We hope you hear both our voices cheering you on.

Delton de Armas
Ocala, Florida

INTRODUCTION

We are careful to be honorable before the Lord,
but we also want everyone else to see that we are
honorable.
—2 Corinthians 8:21

THE ADMINISTRATION AND accounting environment of a nonprofit can be daunting, especially for the uninitiated newcomer. I know this firsthand.

During my first consulting engagement with a church, even with 20 years of experience in corporate accounting and finance, I found the financial statements foreign and intimidating. I hardly knew where to begin. My prior knowledge failed me, and I had no clear resource to turn to for guidance.

Over time, the puzzle pieces started to fit as I guided my first church client through their initial financial audit. The firm they selected had extensive church and nonprofit experience, and their thoughtful questions helped me uncover gaps in my understanding. Each question they asked became an opportunity to learn. The more I learned, the more I realized, *I didn't know what I didn't know.*

In my search for resources, I quickly became frustrated. Most of the available materials I found proved too technical, diving deeply into advanced topics while failing to address the foundational principles. Conversely, some instead proved too simplistic, focusing on the "how" without explaining the "why." What I couldn't find was a practical, straightforward guide—a tool to bridge the gap for accountants unfamiliar with churches or nonprofits, or staff new to accounting. Or perhaps even more common, church and nonprofit staff members intimately familiar with the organization's mission but altogether unfamiliar with accounting.

I needed something to bridge this gap between technical knowledge and mission and ministry know-how.

And so, *The Backoffice Blueprint* was born.

What This Book Is (and Isn't)

This is not a technical manual. You won't find detailed journal entries or complex compliance matrices here. Those belong in the hands of your bookkeeper and CPA.

This is a leadership tool. My goal is to give you the strategic understanding you need to:

1. Ask the right questions about your financial systems
2. Delegate with confidence to financial staff or volunteers
3. Spot risks before they become crises
4. Build systems that support (rather than stifle) your mission

Who Is This Book For?

This book is for executive directors, board members, and ministry leaders who need to understand their organization's financial backbone without becoming accountants themselves.

It's designed for two audiences:

- Accountants stepping into the unique world of church or nonprofit financial management for the first time.

- Church or nonprofit staff tasked with financial or administrative responsibilities, but with little or no formal accounting or administrative training.

If you fall into one of these categories, you are not alone. The journey into church and nonprofit administration often feels overwhelming, but my goal is to make it manageable, practical, and even enjoyable. By the end of this book, you will gain the confidence to navigate the back office with clarity and purpose.

Your Role as a Leader

You don't need to become a financial expert to lead a financially healthy organization. But you do need to understand the terrain.

Think of it like this: a general doesn't need to know how to operate every piece of equipment in the army, but they better understand the strategic capabilities and limitations of their forces. Similarly, you don't need to know how to post journal entries, but you do need to understand what strong financial systems look like and why they matter.

Throughout this book, I'll help you develop what I call "financial fluency"—the ability to have meaningful conversations about your organization's financial health, to ask penetrating questions about your systems, and to make strategic decisions that strengthen rather than undermine your financial foundation.

What Makes This Book Different?

Unlike other church and nonprofit finance resources that either dive too deep into technical waters or barely skim the surface, *The Backoffice Blueprint* builds a framework that's both architecturally sound and practically livable.

First, this guide bridges theory and practice. Instead of handling accounting principles and ministry realities as separate disciplines, we integrate them into a seamless structure. You'll find concrete examples throughout that solidify abstract financial concepts, making them tangible and applicable.

Second, this approach prioritizes prevention over correction, recognizing that retrofitting financial systems costs far more than building them correctly from the start. Well-designed financial processes endure without constant patching or emergency repairs, standing firm through every season of organizational growth.

Third, this blueprint carefully balances detail with accessibility, providing the strategic understanding necessary for sound leadership without overwhelming you with technical jargon. Complex financial topics are explained in clear, straightforward language that serves both financial novices and experienced professionals new to the nonprofit sector.

And finally, I write from a unique vantage point: I've spent years consulting with nonprofits on their financial systems, and my wife and I also run our own ministry. This gives me both the consultant's analytical eye and the practitioner's daily reality check. This book focuses more on the *why* than the *how*, but as a practitioner, the *how* often finds a way to creep in. But know this: I understand it's a journey, not a destination, and I want to be your guide.

The Journey Ahead

In the chapters that follow, we'll walk through each of the five pillars systematically. You'll gain strategic insight into what each pillar accomplishes, why it matters for your mission, and what warning signs suggest weakness in that area.

More importantly, you'll develop the confidence to lead financial conversations rather than simply enduring them. You'll understand not just what your organization should be doing financially, but why these practices matter for your long-term sustainability and impact.

Whether you're leading a grassroots startup or stewarding an established organization, the principles in this book will help you build financial systems worthy of your mission.

Because here's what I've learned after years of working with nonprofits: **The organizations that change the world don't just** have great programs—they have great systems that sustain those programs over time.

Let's build yours.

A Final Word Before We Begin

Financial management in ministry extends far beyond ledgers and spreadsheets. It's about constructing a framework of trust that enables ministry to flourish, while honoring God through excellence in stewardship.

As you work through this material, remember that every financial decision reinforces or weakens the structure you're building. Keep your focus on the larger purpose: creating systems that support and enhance your organization's mission rather than merely complying with technical requirements.

Whether you're breaking ground on new procedures or renovating existing ones, this guide will help you develop a fraud-resistant, ministry-enabling financial framework that serves your organization's vision while maintaining the highest standards of integrity and accountability.

So let's roll up our sleeves and get to work. Your journey toward financial clarity, confidence, and excellence begins now, and the impact of the structure you build will extend far beyond financial statements and policies to transform lives through more effective execution of your organization's vision.

CHAPTER ONE: FOUNDATIONS

"But don't begin until you count the cost. For
who would begin construction of a building without first
calculating the cost to see if there is enough money to
finish it?"
—Luke 14:28 NLT

EVERY ORGANIZATION MUST address foundational housekeeping issues early to set the stage for long-term success. This section isn't just about the *what* or *how*, it's about understanding the *why*. Grasping the purpose behind these practices will empower you to make better decisions and create lasting improvements.

Even if the topics here feel familiar, I encourage you to revisit them with fresh eyes. Without a strong foundation, small errors can snowball into significant challenges over time.

If your organization hasn't fully addressed these foundational steps, don't worry—it's never too late to start. Take this opportunity to identify and correct any deficiencies and commit to a culture of continuous improvement. The journey you embark on now will build a stronger, healthier back office and set your organization on a path to faithful stewardship and excellence.

The Myth: "We're Too Small to Need Systems"

Walk into any struggling nonprofit, and you'll often hear some variation of this refrain: "We're not big enough for formal systems yet." Or: "We can't afford complicated processes." Or my personal favorite: "We're a ministry, not a business."

Here's the truth that took me years to learn: **Strong financial systems don't stifle mission, they fuel it.**

The organizations that change the world aren't the ones with the most charismatic leaders or the flashiest programs. They're the ones that build sustainable systems early, before they need them. They understand that behind every transformational nonprofit is a back office that works, quietly, efficiently, and with integrity.

Consider this: when a donor writes a check to your organization, they're not just supporting your current programs. They're investing in your ability to be good stewards of their resources, to grow wisely, and to sustain impact over time. Every financial decision you make either builds or erodes that trust.

Nonprofit financial management fundamentally differs from business financial management. While businesses pursue profit maximization, nonprofits pursue mission maximization. While businesses measure success by return on investment, nonprofits measure success by return on mission. This difference isn't just philosophical—it shapes every aspect of how your financial systems should be designed and operated.

Yet many nonprofit leaders approach financial management as if they were running a business, adopting systems and practices that optimize for the wrong outcomes. Or, alternatively, they swing too far in the opposite direction, assuming that their noble mission exempts them from rigorous financial practices altogether.

The truth lies somewhere in between. **Your mission doesn't exempt you from financial excellence—it demands it.**

Why Financial Systems Matter for Mission

Every nonprofit leader can tell stories of organizations that started with tremendous vision but collapsed due to financial mismanagement. The founder who commingled personal and organizational funds. The treasurer who "borrowed" money with good intentions but poor documentation. The organization that grew rapidly but never built systems to match their growth.

These aren't stories of bad people. They're stories of good people who underestimated the power of systems.

Consider what strong financial systems actually accomplish for your mission:

They build stakeholder confidence. Donors, board members, and community partners invest not just in your current programs, but in your ability to steward resources wisely over time. Clean audits, timely reports, and transparent practices signal that you take stewardship seriously.

They enable sustainable growth. Organizations with strong systems can scale effectively because they've built infrastructure that supports expansion. They can add new programs, hire additional staff, and pursue larger grants because they've proven they can manage complexity.

They protect against mission drift. When you track resources carefully and report results accurately, you create accountability mechanisms that keep your organization focused on its stated purpose rather than drifting toward whatever seems urgent or easy.

They free leaders to lead. When financial systems work smoothly, leaders can focus on strategy, programs, and relationships rather than constantly fighting financial fires or wondering whether their reports are accurate.

The Five Pillars of Financial Integrity

Throughout my work with both businesses and nonprofits, both as a practitioner and consultant, I've observed that financial health rests on five critical pillars:

1. **Pillar 1: Foundations** — Your legal structure, governance, and basic financial framework that establishes how decisions are made and documented.

2. **Pillar 2: Disbursements** — How you authorize, document, and control money going out, from expense reimbursements to payroll.
3. **Pillar 3: Receipts** — How you receive, acknowledge, and track money coming in, ensuring donor trust and regulatory compliance.
4. **Pillar 4: Financial Reporting & Oversight** — How you transform financial data into actionable intelligence through timely, accurate reporting.
5. **Pillar 5: Implementation** — How you document, train, and sustain these systems through transitions and growth.

Each pillar depends on the others—weakness in one undermines the whole structure. This book provides the strategic framework for understanding all five pillars, while subsequent books in this series will dive deeper into implementing each one.

Most nonprofits excel at one or two of these pillars while neglecting the others. The result? Financial systems that work until they don't. Leaders who understand their programs intimately but feel lost when the treasurer resigns. Organizations that survive crises but never quite thrive.

Think of your nonprofit's financial health as a building supported by five critical pillars. Each pillar serves a distinct function, but they work together to create a stable, sustainable structure:

This book gives you the strategic framework to strengthen all five pillars, not as an accountant would, but as a leader should.

Without thoughtful implementation, policies become mere paperwork, training becomes one-time events, and systems gradually decay until the next crisis forces attention.

The Interconnected Nature of Financial Health

These five pillars don't operate independently—they form an integrated system where weakness in one area undermines the others.

For example, imagine an organization with excellent disbursement controls but weak receipt systems. They might prevent unauthorized spending while simultaneously failing to track donor restrictions properly. The result? Clean expenditure records but restricted funds used inappropriately, leading to donor complaints and potential legal issues.

Or consider an organization that excels at financial reporting but lacks implementation systems. They might produce beautiful monthly reports while having no documented procedures for how those reports get created. When their skilled bookkeeper leaves, the reporting process collapses, leaving leadership flying blind.

The goal isn't perfection in every area immediately, but rather steady progress across all five pillars, with particular attention to addressing your organization's greatest vulnerabilities.

Common Patterns of Financial Weakness

Consider several common patterns that signal systemic financial weakness:

- **The Heroic Individual Pattern:** Everything depends on one person who "knows how everything works." This person might be incredibly competent and well-intentioned, but their departure would create organizational chaos.

- **The Crisis Management Pattern:** Financial attention only emerges during crises—failed audits, cash flow emergencies, or compliance violations.

Between crises, financial systems receive minimal attention.

- **The Growth Outpacing Systems Pattern:** Rapid programmatic growth occurs without corresponding investment in financial infrastructure. Revenue increases but systems don't scale, creating increasing instability.

- **The Compartmentalized Thinking Pattern:** Each pillar develops independently without integration. Strong programs exist alongside weak financial controls, or sophisticated accounting operates without documented procedures.

- **The Compliance-Only Pattern:** Systems focus solely on meeting minimum legal requirements without considering how financial management could support mission effectiveness.

The Characteristics of Financial Health

Financially healthy nonprofits demonstrate several consistent characteristics that transcend specific systems or procedures. These organizations operate with predictable processes where financial activities happen according to documented schedules with clear responsibilities. Month-end closing follows established timelines, and board reports arrive consistently and completely, creating a rhythm of accountability that stakeholders can depend upon.

Communication flows transparently throughout these organizations, with financial information reaching appropriate stakeholders regularly and in formats they can understand and act upon. Board members receive reports that inform rather than confuse, while staff members understand their budgets and spending authority, creating clarity rather than confusion about financial boundaries and expectations.

Perhaps most importantly, these organizations practice proactive problem-solving where issues surface early through regular monitoring rather than remaining hidden until they become crises. Variance reports highlight developing problems while solutions remain available, and leadership addresses concerns before they threaten organizational stability or mission effectiveness.

When growth occurs, it happens sustainably with thoughtful expansion that includes corresponding investment in infrastructure. New programs include appropriate administrative support from the beginning rather than being layered onto already stretched systems, ensuring that growth strengthens rather than weakens the organizational foundation.

Finally, financial stewardship becomes culturally integrated into the organizational DNA rather than remaining merely an administrative function isolated in the back office. All team members understand their role in maintaining financial integrity, from program staff who submit expenses properly to board members who ask thoughtful questions about organizational stewardship.

Your Assessment Starting Point

Before diving into specific pillars, take a moment to assess your organization's current financial health honestly:

- **Foundations:** Do you have current governance documents, appropriate legal status, and basic financial policies? Can new board members quickly understand how financial decisions get made?
- **Disbursements:** Can you explain every payment your organization makes? Do you have controls that would

prevent unauthorized spending while still enabling efficient operations?

- **Receipts:** Do you process donations accurately and provide appropriate acknowledgments? Can you track restricted gifts properly and report on their use?

- **Month-End Closing:** Do you receive accurate financial reports promptly each month? Can your board members understand and act on the financial information they receive?

- **Implementation:** Are your financial procedures documented so they could survive staff transitions? Do team members receive adequate training on financial policies and expectations?

The Path Forward

The remainder of this book will walk through each pillar systematically, giving you the strategic framework to understand what strength looks like in each area and how to build toward it progressively.

Remember: the goal isn't to become a financial expert yourself, but to develop the leadership insight necessary to build systems worthy of your mission. You're not learning to do the work—you're learning to lead the work.

As we explore each pillar, you'll discover that financial excellence isn't about complicated procedures or expensive software. It's about clarity, consistency, and commitment to stewardship that honors both your mission and those who support it.

Strong financial systems don't constrain mission, they support and empower it. Let's build systems that help your organization thrive.

Organizational Structure & Governance

Your organization needs a foundational governance structure that dictates how decisions flow, accountability functions, and leadership operates. Before diving into financial mechanics, establishing this structural framework will significantly impact every aspect of your organization's operation, from legal compliance to day-to-day decision-making.

Think of your organizational structure as the architectural blueprint that determines how your financial building will function: who holds authority to approve expenditures, who bears responsibility for financial oversight, and how resources align with mission. Just as a well-designed building begins with proper engineering plans rather than simply pouring concrete, a sustainable financial system starts with thoughtful governance structures rather than merely setting up bank accounts.

Understanding Legal Requirements

Most states will require you to maintain a minimum board structure to receive and maintain your legal status. While specific requirements vary by state, most jurisdictions typically require you to have at least three people willing to serve as your official board of directors. These board seats will generally include formal titles:

1. **President/Chair** — Provides overall leadership and facilitates board meetings
2. **Secretary** — Maintains organizational records and meeting minutes
3. **Treasurer** — Oversees financial matters and ensures proper stewardship

Required or not, this three-person minimum creates essential checks and balances in organizational governance. While some small organizations might consider having one person hold multiple officer positions to meet statutory requirements, this arrangement undermines the very accountability these positions intend to create.

Articles of Incorporation and Bylaws

Two key documents define your organization's structure and operations:

Think of your **Articles of Incorporation** as your organization's birth certificate. It's the document that officially brings your company to life in the state's eyes. You might also think about your Articles as your organization's *constitution*. Since amending Articles requires filing with state authorities and potentially involves fees, many organizations keep their Articles relatively minimal while addressing more specific operational details in their Bylaws.

Bylaws function as your organization's "operating manual," detailing how leadership structures work in practice. Unlike Articles, you can modify Bylaws without state filings, allowing greater flexibility as your organization matures. Well-crafted Bylaws typically address board composition, officer roles, meeting requirements, decision-making processes, and conflict resolution procedures.

New organizations sometimes assume Bylaws represent mere formality, but they provide crucial guidance during leadership transitions, difficult decisions, or organizational conflicts. Investing in well-crafted Bylaws with legal review may prevent significant challenges later.

Establishing your Tax-Exempt Status

After obtaining your Employer Identification Number (EIN) from the Internal Revenue Service (IRS), you can **apply for tax-exempt status** by filing IRS Form 1023, Application for Recognition of Exemption. This designation not only **confirms** your tax-exempt status but also enables donors to claim tax deductions for their contributions.

The IRS allows 27 months from your organization's formation date to apply, with exemption retroactive to that date. Don't procrastinate! Form 1023 processing can take six months or more, so consider engaging a tax professional with nonprofit experience to assist with the filing.

Choosing the Right Accounting Method

Your choice of accounting method forms a critical design element in your financial structure. You have three basic choices for how you're going to track your money:

Cash-basis accounting tracks revenues and expenses strictly as they flow in and flow out. While straightforward and inherently simple, it harbors weaknesses that can compromise financial reporting reliability, most clearly by not recording future liabilities.

At the opposite end of the spectrum, **accrual accounting** matches revenues and expenses to the period in which they occur. While this *accountant-friendly* method delivers highly accurate financial pictures, so the accountant in me celebrates this approach, it can be overly complex. As a nonprofit leader, even with my training and experience, I understand how its complexity and resource requirements may exceed many organizations' capabilities.

The **modified cash method** combines the simplicity of cash basis with the accuracy of accrual basis for certain key items. Under this method, most income and expenses are recorded when cash changes hands, but significant categories like payroll liabilities, fixed assets, or loans are tracked using accrual adjustments. For many nonprofits, this approach balances ease of use with a clearer financial picture, helping leaders avoid surprises without adding the full complexity of GAAP accrual reporting.

Budgeting Principles

The financial budget serves as the launching pad for effective financial systems. Don't underestimate this process's importance. A budget is a strategic statement of your organization's values and priorities.

A Budget that Reflects Mission

Your budget transcends mere numbers; it embodies a tangible expression of your organization's mission and values. Too many organizations approach budgeting as a financial exercise when it should begin as a missional one. Your budget should flow from your mission and strategic priorities, not from last year's numbers or available funds.

Ground Your Budget in Reality

Base your financial plan on conservative assumptions rather than optimistic projections. Consider using 90% of previous year's income as your planning baseline. This approach avoids presumption and promotes effective stewardship while building resilience into your financial framework. Also consider "funding" depreciation by building reserves into the budget.

Budget Types

Your organization should consider three types of budgets during your annual planning process:

Operating Budget: This is what most people think of when they hear "budget"—your day-to-day income and expenses. It answers the question: "What will we do this year, and how will we pay for it?"

Capital Expenditures Budget: This covers major purchases that will last beyond the current year, such as equipment, vehicles, building improvements, or technology upgrades. It answers the question: "What assets do we need to buy, and where will that money come from?"

Debt Reduction Budget: This shows your plan for paying down existing loans or obligations. It answers the question: "How will we reduce our debt, and which funds will we use?"

Not every organization needs all three budgets, but thinking through these categories helps ensure you're planning comprehensively rather than just focusing on day-to-day operations.

Fiscal Year Strategy

Another important consideration during your organization's initial accounting and administrative setup involves determining your fiscal year. While you can change your fiscal (not *physical*) year-end at any time, establishing it early simplifies operations.

Choosing a Fiscal Year-End

Most organizations default to a calendar year-end of December 31 without much thought. However, selecting a non-calendar fiscal year-end can offer significant advantages, particularly for churches and nonprofits. Many larger organizations already recognize these benefits, operating with fiscal year-ends such as March 31 or September 30. Unfortunately, smaller organizations often stick with the calendar year simply because they don't realize alternatives exist or haven't considered how a different timeline might strengthen their financial foundation.

Advantages of a Non-Calendar Year-End

Choosing a fiscal year that doesn't end on December 31 can reinforce your financial structure in several ways. First, it allows better alignment with your organization's natural giving and spending cycles. Just as a building's design should account for local weather patterns, your financial year can be engineered to match your specific donation rhythms and program schedules.

Second, a non-calendar year-end can create separation between your budgeting process and other time-sensitive year-end responsibilities. This prevents the administrative equivalent of trying to install plumbing and electrical systems simultaneously in the same space—you typically avoid the competing demands of preparing contribution statements and IRS reports (like 1099s and W-2s) while simultaneously planning next year's budget. Note that a March 31 year-end may still create some overlap with tax season preparations, while June 30 or September 30 year-ends provide clearer separation.

Third, scheduling financial audits and other professional services during non-peak periods often results in both cost savings and more attentive service. When auditors aren't juggling dozens of calendar-year clients during tax season, they can dedicate more focus to your organization, not unlike hiring contractors during their off-season.

Disadvantages of a Non-Calendar Year-End

Despite these advantages, using a fiscal year that doesn't align with the calendar does present some challenges to consider. Non-finance staff may find the concept confusing, as most people naturally think in calendar terms. This resembles using metric measurements on a construction site where workers have grown accustomed to standard measurements—it requires additional communication and education.

There are also transition challenges if you decide to switch fiscal years after operating on a calendar basis. Like renovating an existing structure rather than building from scratch, changing your fiscal year after established operations can complicate year-to-year comparisons and require additional explanation to stakeholders.

Selecting the Right Fiscal Year-End

If your organization decides to implement a non-calendar fiscal year, some design choices prove more practical than others. Consider aligning with calendar quarters by selecting a year-end like March 31, June 30, or September 30. This creates a financial framework that's easier for everyone to understand and navigate—where fiscal and calendar quarters align rather than creating odd reporting periods.

Avoid unconventional year-end dates like April 30, which would result in quarters ending in July, October, and January. While not structurally unsound, these unusual patterns create unnecessary complexity for non-financial individuals.

Organizations with affiliated schools might benefit from aligning the fiscal year with the academic calendar, creating natural synchronization between operational and financial cycles.

Whatever fiscal year-end you select, ensure it matches your organization's natural rhythms and administrative patterns. Consistency in application remains essential for creating clarity, both for those working within your financial structure and for outside observers evaluating its integrity as your organization grows.

Segregation of Duties

Segregation of duties transcends mere accounting principle to become a cornerstone of sound financial stewardship. At its core, this practice ensures that no single individual controls all aspects of a financial transaction, creating a framework of checks and balances that protects the organization's resources while building confidence among stakeholders.

This principle divides financial responsibilities into three key activities:

1. **Authorization** of transactions—the approval of expenditures or financial commitments
2. **Recording** of transactions—the documentation and bookkeeping activities
3. **Custody** of assets—the physical or electronic control of funds or property

By dividing these responsibilities among different individuals, you create a structure that minimizes the risk of errors, fraud, or misappropriation. Even the perception of unchecked control can damage trust within your organization.

Implementing Segregation of Duties

Achieving proper segregation can seem challenging for smaller organizations, but thoughtful strategies help maintain strong controls:

- Consider outsourcing key tasks to create separation of functions
- Engage qualified volunteers to help with specific financial duties
- Implement a two-person rule for high-risk activities like counting donations
- Regularly rotate financial roles to maintain fresh perspectives

Data Security

You must also address crucial aspects of data security. Develop a formal IT policy that includes separation of computer-related duties, measures to restrict unauthorized access to sensitive data, strong password requirements, and centralized storage solutions.

Wireless networks represent particularly vulnerable entry points. Avoid unsecured networks and consider establishing what IT professionals call a DMZ—a separate network segment that provides internet access for public users while isolating sensitive internal systems.

Your Financial Foundation

With both human and digital security measures in place, your organization can now focus on the additional financial tools and planning instruments that enhance management capabilities while supporting your mission effectively.

📌 BLUEPRINT NOTE

You now have the strategic framework for understanding your organization's financial health. The five pillars—Foundations, Disbursements, Receipts, Month-End Closing, and Implementation—work together to create a structure that supports rather than stifles your mission. As we dive into each pillar in the following chapters, remember: you're not learning to become an accountant, you're learning to lead with financial confidence. Think of this as your foundation and framing. As you move forward, you'll refine these policies into a complete financial manual.

✅ INSPECTION POINTS

☐ Can you explain how financial systems support (rather than hinder) your mission?

☐ Do you understand the five pillars and how they interconnect?

☐ Do you see yourself as a financial leader (not just a program leader) for your organization?

☐ Is your organization registered with the state and maintaining tax-exempt status?

☐ Have you selected an appropriate accounting method based on your needs?

☐ Does your fiscal year align with your reporting needs and budgeting cycle?

CHAPTER TWO: DISBURSEMENTS & PAYROLL

Good stewardship has less to do with how much is

saved and more to do with how much is not wasted.

—Anthony Coppedge

STEWARDSHIP IS MORE than just a buzzword. It's a lifestyle that the organization models through its financial decisions. Every dollar spent reflects the DNA of the organization, tangibly demonstrating its vision and priorities. Proper stewardship ensures that spending aligns with the collective mission of the organization and its leadership, rather than the preferences of any one individual.

As one pastor-friend wisely observed, "You can tell what is important to a person by looking at his calendar and checkbook." The same is true for organizations. How we allocate resources reveals what we truly value.

Good stewardship is not merely about saving money; it's about avoiding waste. Every expenditure, large or small, should reflect thoughtful, intentional decision-making that advances the organization's mission.

Why Disbursement Controls Matter for Your Mission

Picture this scenario: A well-meaning volunteer writes a $500 check to cover "emergency repairs" without proper authorization. The repair was legitimate, but the vendor was the volunteer's brother-in-law, and the price was inflated. Six months later, during your annual audit, this transaction raises questions about your internal controls and creates doubt about your stewardship practices.

This isn't a story about bad people—it's about weak systems. Without proper disbursement controls, even good intentions can create problems that damage your organization's reputation and mission effectiveness.

Strong disbursement systems deliver on our core principle that systems unleash mission. They do this by ensuring every dollar that leaves your organization advances your purpose while building stakeholder confidence in your stewardship.

When donors, board members, and community partners see that you handle money with appropriate controls and transparency, they're more likely to:

1. Increase their financial support
2. Recommend your organization to others
3. Trust you with larger grants and partnerships
4. Feel confident about your long-term sustainability

The Foundation: Authorization and Documentation

Think of expense authorization as your organization's "permission system." Just as you wouldn't let anyone walk into your building and take equipment, you shouldn't let anyone spend your money without proper approval.

Creating Clear Authorization Levels

Authorization levels establish who can approve different types and amounts of expenditures. Most organizations structure these levels based on dollar amounts and expense categories, creating clear boundaries while enabling efficient operations.

The key is matching approval requirements to organizational risk—routine expenses need streamlined approval, while major commitments require broader input. Your authorization structure should reflect your organization's size, complexity, and risk tolerance.

The Documentation Story

Every payment should tell a complete story that anyone could understand months later. Strong documentation includes the original invoice or receipt, clear business purpose, proper authorization, and appropriate account coding.

The goal isn't bureaucracy—it's accountability. When stakeholders can see exactly how their investments were used to advance your mission, they develop confidence in your stewardship that leads to increased support.

Common Documentation Challenges

Organizations struggle with incomplete documentation, vague expense descriptions, and retroactive approvals. These problems signal weak controls that could undermine stakeholder confidence and create audit issues.

The solution isn't more paperwork—it's clearer expectations and consistent enforcement of documentation standards.

Segregation of Duties: Your Fraud Mitigation System

Here's an uncomfortable truth: most nonprofit fraud isn't committed by strangers—it's done by trusted insiders who gradually realize they can take advantage of weak controls. Segregation of duties helps to protect your organization by ensuring no single person controls all aspects of spending money.

The Three Critical Functions

- **Function 1:** *Authorization* – Who can approve spending?
- **Function 2:** *Processing* – Who actually writes checks or initiates payments?

- **Function 3:** *Reconciliation* – Who verifies that payments were made correctly?

  Ideally, three different people handle these functions. If you can't achieve complete separation, focus on separating the highest-risk combinations:

  Never allow the same person to:

  1. Approve purchases *and* write checks
  2. Manage employment records *and* process and approve payroll
  3. Handle cash receipts *and* reconcile bank accounts

  Example: A small nonprofit discovered their bookkeeper had written $15,000 in unauthorized checks over two years. Simple segregation, such as having the board treasurer review all checks monthly, would likely have caught this in the first month.

Solutions for Small Organizations

Small organizations can maintain effective segregation through creative approaches: involving board members in approval processes, rotating financial responsibilities, using external reviews, or implementing technology solutions that create electronic segregation.

The goal isn't perfect separation—it's reasonable protection given your organizational constraints.

Payroll: Where Complexity Meets Compliance

Payroll represents your organization's most complex and regulated financial activity. Get it wrong, and you'll face penalties, back taxes, and potentially serious legal issues. Get it right, and you demonstrate the kind of operational excellence that builds staff confidence and stakeholder trust.

The Classification Challenge

Many organizations, especially when they are smaller or first getting started, outsource some of their work to vendors, consultants, subcontractors, and independent contractors. The IRS evaluates classification based on behavioral control, financial control, and relationship factors. Worker classification affects tax obligations, benefits, and regulatory compliance.

Misclassification creates significant financial risk through penalties and back-tax obligations. When uncertain, it's generally safer to treat workers, especially individuals, as employees rather than independent contractors.

Essential Documentation and Controls

Proper payroll requires complete personnel files, accurate time records, appropriate approval workflows, and segregation of duties in processing and distribution.

These controls protect both your organization and your employees while ensuring compliance with complex employment regulations.

Technology: Enabler, Not Solution

The right technology can significantly improve disbursement and payroll processes, but technology alone doesn't create good controls—it automates whatever processes you design.

Look for systems that support multiple users with appropriate permissions, maintain detailed audit trails, and integrate with your existing financial infrastructure. Avoid overly complex solutions that require extensive training for basic functions.

Vendor Management

Strong vendor relationships require appropriate oversight through approved vendor lists, competitive bidding for major purchases, and regular review of recurring services. Document your vendor approval process and ensure multiple people understand key vendor relationships.

Credit Card Controls

Credit cards offer convenience but require strict controls: written policies on acceptable use, individual cards rather than shared accounts, monthly reconciliation by someone other than the cardholder, and regular review of all charges by leadership.

Building Sustainable Disbursement Systems

Strong disbursement systems aren't just about policies and procedures—they're about creating organizational culture that values stewardship and accountability.

This requires leadership modeling appropriate behavior, clear communication about why controls matter, and regular review of systems as your organization grows. The goal is building financial integrity that becomes part of your organizational DNA rather than just administrative requirements.

✒ BLUEPRINT NOTE

Strong disbursement and payroll systems deliver on our core principle: they ensure every dollar leaving your organization advances your mission while building stakeholder confidence in your stewardship. These aren't just administrative requirements—they're the operational foundation that enables sustainable growth and mission impact.

☑ INSPECTION POINTS

☐ Do you have clear, written authorization levels that staff actually follow?

☐ Can you explain every payment your organization makes with proper documentation?

☐ Are financial responsibilities divided among multiple people to help prevent fraud?

☐ Do you properly classify and document all workers (employees vs. contractors)?

☐ Are payroll processes accurate, compliant, and properly controlled?

CHAPTER THREE: RECEIPTS & REVENUE INTEGRITY

NOW THAT WE'VE established your organizational foundation, we turn to the operational heart of your financial systems: how money flows in and out of your organization. The next two chapters explore disbursements and receipts—the daily financial activities that either build or erode stakeholder trust.

Ensuring Proper Handling of Donations

As a building needs proper entry points to welcome visitors, your organization's financial structure requires carefully designed inflow systems for donations. Money flowing into your organization represents more than financial transactions. It reflects the trust, generosity, and commitment of those who believe in your mission. How you handle these contributions directly impacts donor confidence, regulatory compliance, and your organization's long-term sustainability.

Strong receipt systems enable and empower leaders to deliver on their mission. They demonstrate stewardship, build donor relationships, ensure legal compliance, and create the foundation for sustainable growth. When stakeholders see that contributions are handled with integrity and transparency, they're more likely to give again and recommend your organization to others.

This chapter addresses the strategic principles behind effective revenue management—from physical donation handling to electronic giving platforms, from donor acknowledgment requirements to restricted fund management. By the end, you'll understand how to build systems that protect both your organization and your donors while positioning your nonprofit for growth.

Why Receipt Integrity Matters for Your Mission

Consider this scenario: A major donor visits your organization and witnesses volunteers casually handling cash donations without proper controls. Later, they discover their restricted gift was used for general operations rather than the specified program. What started as enthusiasm for your mission becomes doubt about your competence and integrity.

This isn't just about preventing theft—though that's important. It's about building the institutional credibility that enables sustainable funding. Donors don't just give to causes they believe in; they give to organizations they trust to steward their investments effectively.

When donors see professional handling of their contributions, they experience confidence in your organization's overall management. This confidence translates into:

- Increased giving levels over time
- Referrals to other potential supporters
- Willingness to make major or planned gifts
- Advocacy for your organization in the community
- Patience during challenging seasons

Conversely, poor receipt handling creates doubt that extends beyond financial management to questions about your organization's professionalism, sustainability, and even worse, credibility.

The Foundation of Donor Trust

Every donation represents a relationship. Whether someone drops a check in the offering plate or sets up recurring electronic giving, they're making a statement about their confidence in your organization's mission and management.

Strong receipt systems communicate several important messages to donors:

- **Competence:** You can manage resources effectively and professionally
- **Integrity:** You handle funds with appropriate care and oversight
- **Transparency:** You account for every dollar and use it as intended
- **Respect:** You value both the gift and the giver

These perceptions directly impact donor retention, referrals, and long-term giving patterns. Organizations with strong receipt systems consistently outperform those with weak systems in donor retention and average gift size.

The Modern Revenue Landscape

Today's nonprofit revenue management involves complexity previous generations never faced. Organizations must navigate multiple giving channels, evolving donor expectations, changing regulations, and sophisticated fraud schemes.

Revenue Stream Diversification

Modern nonprofits typically receive income through various channels:

- **Traditional donations** (cash, checks, planned gifts)
- **Electronic giving** (online platforms, mobile apps, text giving)

- **Grant funding** (foundations, government, corporate)
- **Earned revenue** (fees for service, product sales)
- **Special events** (galas, auctions, fundraising campaigns)

Each revenue stream requires different handling procedures, compliance requirements, and relationship management approaches. The challenge isn't mastering every technical detail—it's building systems robust enough to handle this complexity while maintaining donor trust.

Regulatory Complexity

Nonprofit revenue management occurs within a web of federal, state, and local regulations:

- **IRS requirements** for contribution acknowledgments and reporting
- **State registration** requirements for charitable solicitation
- **Payment processing** regulations for electronic transactions
- **Data privacy** laws affecting donor information management
- **Employment regulations** for fundraising staff

These requirements continue evolving, making professional guidance essential for ongoing compliance.

Physical Donation Handling

Despite the growth of electronic giving, most nonprofits still receive significant physical donations that require careful handling.

The Two-Person Rule

The foundation of secure donation handling is simple: never allow a single person to count money alone. This protects both your organization and your volunteers from suspicion or false accusations.

A counting policy requiring two unrelated persons, that is, two individuals who do not have a family, business, or personal relationship, prevents problems by creating accountability for everyone involved, providing immediate verification of amounts, eliminating opportunities for misappropriation, and protecting volunteers from false accusations.

This rule applies regardless of the amounts involved or the trustworthiness of individuals. It's about creating systems that protect everyone while building institutional credibility.

Security Throughout the Process

Physical donations require careful handling from collection through deposit. Your procedures should address:

- **Collection protocols** that maintain security during services or events
- **Counting procedures** that ensure accuracy while preventing loss
- **Storage requirements** that protect funds until deposit
- **Deposit procedures** that minimize risk while maintaining efficiency

The goal isn't elaborate security measures—it's reasonable protection that demonstrates appropriate stewardship of donor investments.

Common Physical Handling Challenges

Organizations struggle with balancing security and efficiency, managing volunteer involvement, handling unusual gifts (like foreign currency or bonds), and maintaining procedures during busy periods or special events.

Effective systems anticipate these challenges and provide clear guidance for handling exceptions while maintaining security standards.

Electronic Giving Systems

Electronic giving has transformed nonprofit fundraising, with many organizations now receiving 50% or more of their donations through electronic channels. This shift offers advantages for both organizations and donors but requires different controls and procedures.

The Digital Transformation

Electronic giving provides benefits that traditional methods can't match:

- **Convenience** for donors who prefer digital transactions
- **Recurring giving** capabilities that improve cash flow predictability
- **Reduced processing costs** compared to check handling
- **Better tracking** and reporting capabilities
- **Global reach** for organizations with dispersed constituencies

However, electronic systems also introduce new risks around data security, transaction fees, platform reliability, and regulatory compliance.

Platform Selection Considerations

Choosing the right electronic giving platform requires careful consideration of multiple factors:

- **Security requirements** that protect donor information and prevent fraud
- **Integration capabilities** with existing donor management systems
- **Fee structures** that balance cost with functionality
- **User experience** that encourages rather than discourages giving
- **Reporting capabilities** that support stewardship and compliance

The goal isn't finding the cheapest option—it's selecting platforms that build donor confidence while supporting your organizational needs.

New Giving Methods

Today's donors expect multiple ways to give:

- **Online forms** integrated with organizational websites
- **Mobile apps** optimized for smartphone use
- **Text giving** for immediate, impulse donations
- **Social media** integration for peer-to-peer fundraising
- **Cryptocurrency** options for tech-savvy donors

Each method requires different technical infrastructure and compliance considerations.

Donor Acknowledgment and Compliance

Proper donor acknowledgment serves dual purposes: regulatory compliance and relationship building. Getting this right demonstrates professionalism while strengthening donor connections.

IRS Requirements

The IRS has specific requirements for contribution acknowledgments that affect both your organization and your donors. For contributions of $250 or more, donors must receive written acknowledgment from your organization to claim a tax deduction.

Beyond basic compliance, acknowledgment timing and quality affect donor perception of your organization's professionalism and appreciation.

Building Donor Relationships

Contribution acknowledgments serve purposes beyond tax compliance—they're opportunities to strengthen donor relationships and communicate impact. Well-crafted acknowledgments express genuine gratitude, reinforce mission connection, and encourage continued engagement.

The best acknowledgments make donors feel valued as partners in your mission rather than just sources of funding.

Acknowledgment Challenges

Organizations struggle with timely acknowledgment processing, personalizing communications for different donor segments, managing acknowledgments for recurring gifts, and balancing automation with personal touch.

Effective systems address these challenges through clear procedures, appropriate technology, and regular quality review.

Restricted and Designated Funds

Understanding and managing donor restrictions represents one of the most complex aspects of nonprofit revenue management. Mistakes in this area can damage donor relationships and create legal obligations.

Understanding the Distinction

Many nonprofit leaders confuse designated funds with restricted funds, but the distinction has important legal and practical implications:

Designated funds are created by board action and can be reallocated if circumstances change. The board maintains ultimate authority over these resources.

Restricted funds are created by donor stipulations and carry legal obligations. Organizations must use these funds exactly as donors specify or return them.

This distinction affects everything from budgeting to financial reporting to donor communications.

The Challenge of Restricted Gifts

Restricted gifts require careful consideration before acceptance. Leadership should evaluate alignment with mission, assess feasibility of meeting restrictions, and document agreements clearly with donors.

Some restrictions create more problems than benefits:

- **Overly specific** restrictions that limit flexibility
- **Time-sensitive** restrictions that create operational challenges
- **Conflicting** restrictions that contradict existing commitments
- **Insufficient** restricted amounts that don't cover full program costs

The key is thoughtful evaluation before acceptance rather than accepting all gifts without consideration.

Managing Donor Intent

Effective restricted fund management requires clear systems for:

- **Documenting** donor intentions accurately
- **Tracking** restricted funds separately from general operations
- **Reporting** to donors on how their restricted gifts are used
- **Communicating** with donors when circumstances change

This isn't just about compliance—it's about maintaining the trust relationships that enable future giving.

Example: A Cautionary Tale

The risks of donor-restricted funds stand starkly illustrated by a real-life example:

A church once received a $1,000,000 restricted gift to purchase an organ. After the donor passed away, the church decided to shift its priorities and concluded that buying an organ no longer aligned with its mission. However, the donor's heirs refused to release the restriction, leveraging it to increase their inheritance. Unable to resolve the issue legally, the church had to return the $1,000,000 donation. The church believed the donor intended to support their ministry, not specifically the organ, but the donor's inability to release the restriction led to lost opportunities to grow the church—like being forced to install a specific feature in your building that no longer serves your needs.

Data Security and Privacy

Modern revenue management involves collecting, storing, and processing sensitive donor information. Protecting this data isn't just good practice—it's a legal requirement and trust imperative.

Information at Risk

Donor databases contain valuable information including:

- **Personal details** (names, addresses, phone numbers)
- **Financial information** (giving history, payment methods)
- **Preference data** (communication preferences, interests)
- **Relationship information** (connections to other donors, involvement history)

This information attracts both criminal activity and competitive intelligence gathering.

Security Responsibilities

Organizations must balance accessibility with security:

- **Access controls** that limit who can view sensitive information
- **Backup systems** that protect against data loss
- **Update procedures** that maintain data accuracy
- **Disposal protocols** that properly destroy outdated information

The goal isn't fortress-like security that prevents normal operations—it's reasonable protection that demonstrates appropriate stewardship of donor trust.

Revenue Recognition Complexities

Not all money received by nonprofits represents the same type of revenue. Understanding these distinctions affects financial reporting, tax obligations, and donor communications.

Types of Revenue

Nonprofits typically receive several types of income:
- **Contributions** (donations with no expectation of return)
- **Grants** (restricted funding for specific purposes)
- **Earned revenue** (payment for goods or services)
- **Investment income** (returns on organizational investments)

Each type has different accounting treatment, reporting requirements, and tax implications.

Recognition Timing

When to recognize revenue depends on several factors:
- **Unconditional vs. conditional** gifts
- **Restricted vs. unrestricted** funds
- **Cash vs. pledged** contributions
- **Current vs. future** use requirements

Understanding these distinctions helps organizations report accurately and communicate effectively with donors.

Building Sustainable Revenue Systems

Effective receipt systems aren't just about preventing problems—they're about creating infrastructure that supports organizational growth and mission advancement.

Scalability Considerations

Revenue systems must grow with your organization:
- **Volume handling** that accommodates increasing donation levels
- **Complexity management** as revenue streams diversify
- **Staff transitions** that preserve institutional knowledge
- **Technology upgrades** that maintain security and efficiency

The goal is building systems that strengthen rather than strain under growth pressures.

Continuous Improvement

Revenue systems require ongoing attention and refinement:
- **Regular assessment** of current practices and results
- **Stakeholder feedback** from donors, staff, and volunteers
- **Technology updates** to maintain security and functionality
- **Procedure refinement** based on experience and changing needs

This isn't about constant change—it's about thoughtful evolution that maintains effectiveness while adapting to new circumstances.

Integration with Overall Financial Management

Receipt systems don't operate in isolation—they must integrate smoothly with your organization's broader financial management:
- **Accounting systems** that accurately record and track donations

- **Budgeting processes** that reflect realistic revenue projections
- **Financial reporting** that demonstrates stewardship to stakeholders
- **Audit preparation** that provides necessary documentation

Effective integration ensures that revenue management supports rather than complicates overall financial health.

📌 BLUEPRINT NOTE

Your receipt and revenue integrity systems form the trust foundation of your financial structure. By establishing secure collection processes, proper donor acknowledgment procedures, and effective fund management practices, you create a framework that protects resources while building lasting donor relationships. Remember: every donation represents both a financial transaction and a relationship opportunity.

✅ INSPECTION POINTS

☐ Do you have secure procedures for handling all types of donations?

☐ Are donor acknowledgments timely, compliant, and relationship-building?

☐ Do you understand the difference between restricted and designated funds?

☐ Are electronic giving systems secure and user-friendly?

☐ Can you properly track and report on restricted fund usage?

CHAPTER FOUR: FINANCIAL REPORTING

Numbers alone mean little, just as words out of

context mean little. It's the story that counts. In

financial reporting, reading numbers is looking for the

plot, the story of where the cash is flowing.

—Robert T. Kiyosaki (Rich Dad Poor Dad)

YOU'VE ESTABLISHED YOUR foundations, built controls for money going out and coming in, and created systems that protect your organization's resources. Now comes a critical question: how do you transform all this financial activity into the strategic intelligence that drives effective leadership and builds stakeholder confidence?

Month-end closing and financial reporting represent far more than accounting exercises. They create the foundation for informed leadership, early problem detection, and confident board governance. When done well, they transform your organization's financial data into the strategic intelligence you need to lead effectively.

What story does your organization's financial data tell? Every month, thousands of individual transactions flow through your systems—donations received, expenses paid, programs delivered, people served. But without disciplined processes to transform this raw data into meaningful reports, these transactions remain just numbers in a ledger rather than strategic intelligence that drives mission-focused decisions.

This chapter explores both the process of month-end closing and the financial statements that result from it—showing you how to build systems that serve leadership rather than just satisfy compliance requirements.

The Strategic Value of Financial Reporting

Most nonprofit leaders see month-end closing as a necessary burden—something the bookkeeper handles while everyone else focuses on "real" work. This perspective misses the strategic value that well-designed financial reporting can provide.

Consider what happens in organizations with weak financial reporting versus those with strong systems:

Weak Systems: Board members receive numbers they can't understand or act upon. Budget variances go unexplained until small problems become major crises. Leadership makes decisions based on outdated information.

Strong Systems: Financial reports arrive promptly and tell a clear story about organizational health. Board meetings focus on strategy rather than deciphering numbers. Budget variances are identified and addressed before they become problems.

The difference isn't just about having better numbers—it's about creating the information foundation that enables effective leadership.

Building Your Closing Process

Creating effective month-end closing procedures requires understanding what you're trying to accomplish and designing processes that serve your organization's specific needs.

The Foundation: Daily Processing Excellence

Month-end closing problems usually stem from daily processing weaknesses. You can't create accurate monthly reports from inaccurate daily transactions. Strong closing processes begin with disciplined daily financial management.

Essential Closing Components

While every organization's closing process differs, certain elements remain consistently important:

- **Account reconciliation** ensures your records match external sources
- **Review and analysis** of results identifies unusual items and potential errors
- **Documentation and approval** create accountability and provide evidence of proper procedures

Understanding Your Financial Statements

The ultimate output of your month-end closing process is a set of three financial statements that work together to tell your organization's complete financial story. The statement of financial position, or balance sheet, shows your current position. The statement of activities, or income statement, explains your performance. And the cash flow statement ties the two together, revealing how your cash actually moved. Together, they give you the information needed for informed leadership decisions. Let's look at them one at a time.

The Statement of Financial Position (Balance Sheet)

Think of your Statement of Financial Position as a snapshot of your organization's financial health at a specific moment in time. It shows what you own (assets), what you owe (liabilities), and what remains (net assets).

The Statement of Activities

Your Statement of Activities shows your organization's financial performance over a period of time. (Accountants might know or refer to this by other names like "Income Statement" or "Statement of Revenue and Expenses," but the concept remains the same.) Unlike businesses that focus on profit maximization, nonprofits use this statement to demonstrate how effectively they're using resources to advance their mission. This statement also shows the change in your organization's net assets— essentially whether you ended the year financially stronger or weaker than when you started.

The Statement of Cash Flows

Often the most overlooked financial statement, the cash flow statement bridges the gap between your balance sheet and income statement by showing how cash actually moved through your organization during the reporting period. Think of it as the Balance Sheet over time.

Creating Board-Ready Reports

Financial statements serve different audiences with different needs. Board members need strategic insights, not accounting detail. Your reporting should help trustees understand organizational health and make informed governance decisions.

Key Performance Indicators

Focus on metrics that matter for mission effectiveness:

- **Liquidity indicators** show whether your organization can meet short-term obligations

- **Efficiency indicators** demonstrate how well you're using resources
- **Growth indicators** reveal sustainability trends

Common Closing Challenges and Solutions

Most organizations face predictable challenges in developing effective closing processes:

The "Perfect Information" Trap

Some organizations delay closing while pursuing every minor adjustment. The solution: Accept that *monthly* reports provide management information, not audit-level precision, while annual reports require much more care.

The "One-Person Show" Problem

Many organizations have one person handling all closing procedures. The solution: Involve multiple people in appropriate roles with proper review procedures.

The Payoff: Strategic Financial Intelligence

Organizations with effective financial reporting operate differently from those with weak processes. They make decisions based on current information, identify problems early, and build stakeholder confidence through consistent, reliable reporting.

This operational advantage translates directly into mission impact. When you can trust your financial reports, you can focus on programs rather than wondering about numbers.

Building Trust Through Transparent Accountability

Your organization's external financial reporting tells an important story: how you're fulfilling your public trust as a tax-exempt organization. Unlike internal reports designed for operational decision-making, external reporting serves multiple stakeholders—donors, government agencies, and community members who expect transparency about your impact and stewardship.

The Strategic Value of External Compliance

Many nonprofit leaders view external reporting requirements as burdensome overhead. This perspective misses the strategic advantages that thoughtful external reporting can provide:

Trust Building: Transparent financial reporting builds confidence among donors, volunteers, and community partners

Operational Discipline: External reporting requirements force organizations to maintain accurate records, document decisions, and follow consistent procedures throughout the year.

Risk Management: Regular compliance activities help identify potential problems before they become serious issues.

Access to Opportunities: Many grant-making foundations require current Form 990s and audited financial statements before considering funding proposals.

Board Oversight: The Governance Foundation

Effective external reporting begins with strong board governance. Your board serves as the bridge between internal operations and external accountability, ensuring that financial reporting meets both legal requirements and stakeholder expectations.

Establishing Oversight Responsibilities

Board members have legal fiduciary responsibilities that extend beyond approving budgets and reviewing monthly reports. They must ensure the organization complies with all applicable regulations, maintains appropriate controls, and reports accurately to external stakeholders.

This doesn't require board members to become accountants, but it does require them to ask thoughtful questions about confidence in numbers, controls that ensure accuracy, and whether reports clearly communicate mission impact.

Form 990: Your Annual Public Report

The IRS Form 990 serves as much more than a tax filing—it's your organization's primary public disclosure document. Anyone can access your Form 990 through websites like GuideStar or Charity Navigator, making it a critical tool for public accountability and stakeholder communication.

Strategic Preparation Throughout the Year

The worst time to think about Form 990 preparation is when it's due. Organizations that treat Form 990 as an annual crisis inevitably produce lower-quality filings that miss opportunities to communicate effectively about their work.

Instead, use Form 990 requirements as a framework for organizing information throughout the year. Maintain board meeting minutes consistently, document significant program activities as they occur, and track governance compliance systematically. Form 990 requirements and deadlines are updated regularly by the IRS, so work with your tax professional to ensure compliance with current requirements.

Leveraging Form 990 for Communication

Thoughtful organizations use Form 990 as a powerful communication tool. The organization description sections allow you to tell your mission story in your own words. Remember that potential donors, grant-makers, and community partners often review Form 990s before deciding whether to support your work. Rather than viewing Form 990 as a compliance burden, treat it as an annual opportunity to showcase your organization's impact and stewardship.

External Audits and Reviews

External audits provide independent verification of your financial statements and internal controls. While not all organizations are required to have audits, many find them valuable for building stakeholder confidence and identifying improvement opportunities.

The Key Difference: Trust vs. Verify

Many people use the term "audit" when they actually mean "review," but there's an important distinction. A **review** asks management questions and performs basic analytical procedures—essentially taking your word for what happened while checking that it makes sense. An **audit** goes much further by independently verifying your assertions with supporting evidence—they don't just ask if you have proper controls, they test them to make sure they actually work.

Think of it this way: a review is like having someone look at your financial statements and ask, "Does this seem reasonable?" An audit is like having someone say, "Show me the receipts, bank statements, and procedures that prove this is accurate."

Understanding Requirements

Audit and review requirements vary by state, organizational size, and funding sources. Beyond formal requirements, consider whether enhanced assurance makes strategic sense for your organization. Both build credibility with major donors and foundations, provide objective assessment of financial practices, and can identify problems before they become serious issues.

Preparing for Audit Success

Audit and Review costs and effectiveness depend largely on how well you prepare. Organizations with clean, organized records and documented procedures make audits run smoothly and cost-effectively.

State and Local Compliance

Tax-exempt status with the IRS doesn't eliminate all other regulatory requirements. Most nonprofits must also comply with state and local regulations that vary significantly by location and organizational type.

State Registration Requirements

Most states require charitable organizations to register before soliciting donations within their borders. Registration isn't just about initial filing; it requires ongoing compliance with annual reports and fee payments.

Employment and Payroll Compliance

Tax-exempt status doesn't exempt organizations from employment law requirements. You must still comply with federal and state payroll tax obligations, unemployment insurance requirements, and wage and hour regulations.

Building a Culture of Compliance

Effective external reporting isn't just about following rules—it's about building organizational culture that values transparency, accuracy, and accountability in all financial activities.

Integration with Daily Operations

The most successful compliance programs integrate requirements into daily operations rather than treating them as separate activities. When staff understand how their daily work contributes to external reporting accuracy, they're more likely to maintain high standards consistently.

Continuous Improvement

Treat external reporting as an opportunity for organizational learning and improvement. Use audit findings as a roadmap for strengthening internal controls. Review stakeholder feedback to identify communication improvements.

Balancing Compliance and Mission

Remember that compliance serves mission rather than replacing it. The goal isn't perfect paperwork—it's sustainable stewardship that enables effective ministry. When compliance requirements seem to conflict with mission activities, look for creative solutions that honor both obligations.

📌 BLUEPRINT NOTE

Your month-end closing and financial reporting processes transform raw transaction data into the strategic intelligence that drives effective leadership. By building disciplined procedures that produce timely, accurate, and meaningful reports, you create the foundation for informed decision-making and confident governance. Remember: financial statements tell your organization's story—make sure it's a story worth telling.

☑ INSPECTION POINTS

☐ Are your financial reports produced timely and tell a clear story about organizational performance?

☐ Can board members understand and act upon the financial reports they receive?

☐ Are budget variances analyzed and addressed rather than just reported?

☐ Does your board understand its fiduciary responsibilities for external reporting oversight?

☐ Do you understand which audit or compliance requirements apply to your organization?

☐ Are you using financial reporting as a strategic tool rather than just meeting compliance requirements?

CHAPTER FIVE: IMPLEMENTATION

The important thing is that you've got a strong foundation before you start to try to save the world or help other people.

—Richard Branson

YOU'VE LAID A strong financial foundation, built fraud-resistant systems, and established clear reporting and oversight procedures. But financial health doesn't just depend on setting up the right processes—it thrives through sustaining them over time.

This section focuses on implementation:

- Documenting your financial policies into a comprehensive financial manual
- Training staff and leadership on their financial responsibilities and accountability
- Leveraging software & technology to streamline operations and improve accuracy
- Establishing ongoing internal review & accountability to prevent breakdowns

A financial system succeeds only as well as its execution. Without clear documentation, training, and accountability, even the best-designed processes will eventually fail. This final section ensures that your financial systems don't just exist on paper but become a living framework—one that protects, sustains, and empowers your ministry for years to come.

With strong controls in place for money coming in and going out, we now address how to transform all this financial activity into meaningful intelligence. Financial reporting and oversight aren't just about compliance—they're about telling your organization's story in ways that build confidence and enable strategic decisions.

Building Systems That Last

Picture this: Carol has been your organization's unofficial financial guru for fifteen years. She knows every donor story, every fund restriction, every quirky procedure that keeps things running smoothly. Then one day, Carol announces her retirement. Suddenly, you realize that your organization's financial knowledge is walking out the door.

This scenario haunts nonprofit leaders everywhere: the recognition that critical organizational knowledge lives in someone's head rather than in documented systems. But here's the uncomfortable truth: even the most brilliantly designed financial systems fail if they aren't properly implemented and sustained.

The Implementation Challenge

Why do so many well-intentioned financial improvements fail to stick? The answer usually isn't technical, it's cultural. Organizations often approach financial systems like construction projects: design the blueprint, install the components, and declare victory. But financial systems are living frameworks that require ongoing attention, adaptation, and buy-in from everyone who interacts with them.

The "Carol Problem" represents the situation where critical knowledge exists only in institutional memory, creating crises through transition.

The "Shelf-ware Problem" occurs when organizations invest in creating policies and procedures that end up gathering dust... beautiful manuals that nobody reads!

The **"Compliance Theater Problem"** happens when organizations go through the motions of following procedures without understanding their purpose.

Successful implementation addresses all three problems by creating systems that are documented, accessible, and meaningful to the people who use them.

Documentation: Beyond the Manual

Everyone knows they should document their financial procedures, but most organizations approach documentation as a necessary evil rather than a strategic tool. Effective documentation serves multiple purposes: it preserves institutional knowledge, ensures consistency, enables training, and provides accountability.

Think about the difference between a cookbook and a chemistry textbook. Both contain detailed instructions, but only one is designed for practical application. Your financial documentation should be more cookbook than textbook—focused on helping people accomplish specific tasks with measurable outcomes.

Key Documentation Principles:

- Start with critical processes that pose the highest risk if performed incorrectly
- Use multiple formats to accommodate different learning styles
- Make it findable when people need it
- Keep it current through regular review and updates

Training: Creating Competence, Not Just Compliance

Most organizations approach financial training as an onboarding process and maybe they review procedures annually.

Then hope for the best. This approach treats training as information transfer rather than creating competency.

Effective training creates understanding, not just awareness. Instead of simply explaining what to do, help people understand why procedures exist and how they contribute to organizational success.

Building Training That Works:

- Address different learning needs within your organization
- Create ongoing learning opportunities rather than just initial training
- Build internal expertise so you're not dependent on external consultants
- Connect procedures to mission impact

Technology: Strategic Enabler, Not Silver Bullet

Technology can dramatically improve financial management, but only when it's properly implemented and integrated into organizational workflows. Too many organizations invest in sophisticated software only to discover that people continue using manual workarounds because the technology wasn't properly integrated into their culture and processes.

Strategic Technology Considerations

The right financial technology should support your procedures, not determine or undermine them. Before selecting any system, understand your current processes and identify specific problems technology could solve. Technology implementation requires change management, not just technical installation.

Key Evaluation Criteria:

- **Integration capabilities** - Will it work with your existing systems?
- **Scalability** - Can it grow with your organization?
- **User adoption** - Is it intuitive enough for your team to actually use?
- **Support and training** - What happens when you need help?
- **Total cost of ownership** - Beyond initial purchase, what are ongoing costs?

Common Technology Mistakes to Avoid

Don't choose systems based solely on features or price. The most sophisticated system is worthless if your team won't use it. Similarly, the cheapest option may cost more in the long run if it can't support your needs as you grow.

Avoid "shiny object syndrome" - constantly switching systems in search of the perfect solution. Stability and consistency often matter more than having the latest features.

Building Internal Capability

Plan for the full lifecycle of technology implementation, including training, data migration, and ongoing support. Build internal expertise so you're not completely dependent on external consultants for basic functions.

Remember: technology should make your financial processes more efficient and reliable, not more complicated. If a system isn't solving real problems or improving actual outcomes, it's not the right choice for your organization.

Culture Change: The Hidden Success Factor

The most overlooked aspect of implementation is culture change. Financial systems don't exist in isolation—they're part of how your organization operates, makes decisions, and pursues its mission.

Reliable financial reporting is more than an administrative discipline; it reflects an organization's values. When stewardship is woven into the culture, financial data becomes a tool for clarity and decision-making rather than a compliance exercise. Leaders engage with reports as a way to align resources with mission, not as a distraction from the work.

Without this cultural shift, even the best-designed systems can fail to take root. Reports may be generated but ignored, variances explained but never addressed, and data reduced to static snapshots rather than catalysts for strategy. A culture that values stewardship ensures that financial reporting leads to action and builds trust throughout the organization.

Addressing Cultural Factors:

- Address resistance directly and empathetically
- Connect financial procedures to mission impact
- Celebrate improvements and successes
- Learn from mistakes without blame

Building Implementation Momentum

Successful implementation rarely happens all at once. Instead, it requires building momentum through small wins, consistent execution, and ongoing adaptation based on experience.

Start with high-impact, low-complexity improvements that demonstrate value quickly. This might mean implementing a simple approval workflow, standardizing bank reconciliation procedures, or creating basic financial reports. Early wins build confidence and support for more complex improvements.

Communicate progress and plans regularly to maintain organizational support. People need to understand not just what's changing but why it's changing and how it will benefit them and the organization. Regular communication prevents rumors and builds confidence in the implementation process.

Measure and monitor key indicators of implementation success. This might include time required for financial processes, error rates in key procedures, timeliness of financial reports, or staff satisfaction with new systems. Use these metrics to identify areas needing attention and celebrate improvements.

Adapt based on experience rather than rigidly following initial plans. Implementation often reveals unexpected challenges or opportunities that require adjustments. The goal is creating systems that work, not following predetermined procedures regardless of their effectiveness.

Sustaining Systems Over Time

Creating effective financial systems is challenging, but sustaining them over time can be even more difficult. Organizations change, staff turn over, and external requirements evolve.

Sustainability Factors:

- Plan for transitions before they occur
- Stay current with best practices through professional development
- Conduct regular reviews of your financial systems
- Invest in ongoing capability building

The Leadership Imperative

Successful implementation requires active leadership support, not just passive approval. Leaders must champion financial systems, model appropriate behavior, and create the conditions for success.

Leadership Responsibilities:

- Model the behavior you expect
- Provide necessary resources for implementation success
- Create accountability without micromanagement
- Communicate the vision of excellent financial management

Implementation as Ongoing Process

Perhaps the most important insight about implementation is that it's not a one-time project but an ongoing process. Financial systems are living frameworks that require continuous attention, adaptation, and improvement.

The organizations that succeed long-term are those that view implementation as creating competency rather than task completion. They create systems that learn and adapt, build internal expertise that grows over time, and maintain flexibility to respond to changing circumstances.

✒ BLUEPRINT NOTE

Implementation transforms financial blueprints into living systems that serve your organization's mission. Success requires more than good procedures—it demands thoughtful documentation, effective training, appropriate technology, and culture change that aligns financial practices with organizational values. Remember: systems that work regardless of who's in charge are systems that truly serve your mission.

☑ INSPECTION POINTS

☐ Are your financial procedures documented in ways that enable effective training and transitions?

☐ Do staff members understand both the "how" and "why" of financial procedures?

☐ Does your technology support your procedures rather than determining them?

☐ Have you addressed cultural resistance to financial procedures with empathy and clear communication?

☐ Are you building internal capability rather than remaining dependent on external experts?

☐ Do you have transition plans that preserve institutional knowledge when staff members leave?

☐ Do leaders model the financial behavior they expect from others?

☐ Do you treat implementation as an ongoing process rather than a one-time project?

CHAPTER SIX: BUILDING YOUR BLUEPRINT

Ideas are easy. Implementation is hard.

—Guy Kawasaki

YOU'VE DESIGNED THE systems, but design without implementation is merely good intentions. This final chapter ensures your financial systems become living, breathing practices that sustain your organization through growth and transitions.

A Strategic Framework For Financial Transformation

You've reached the point where knowledge meets action. You know what to do, and now you need to do it. We have covered the five pillars of financial health. You've seen why each matters for your mission, and you've learned how successful organizations implement lasting change. Now comes the crucial question: where do you start?

This chapter provides a strategic framework for assessing your organization's current state, prioritizing improvements, and creating a roadmap that fits your unique situation. The most successful financial transformations happen when leaders think strategically rather than tactically.

The Assessment Imperative

Picture this: You wouldn't start a construction project without surveying the building site. You wouldn't plan a trip without knowing your starting point. Yet many nonprofit leaders jump into financial improvements without understanding their current reality.

Honest assessment isn't about finding fault—it's about gaining clarity. Before you can build anything meaningful, you need to know your organization's current financial capabilities, identify gaps between where you are and where you need to be, and recognize opportunities for improvement that will have the greatest impact on your mission.

Most organizations skip this crucial step, jumping straight into solutions without understanding their problems. The result? Improvements that don't stick, resources invested in the wrong areas, and frustration when change doesn't deliver expected results.

Your assessment needs to answer three critical questions:

1. **Where are we strongest?** (What's already working that we can build on?)
2. **Where are we most vulnerable?** (What poses the greatest risk to our mission?)
3. **Where can we get the biggest impact for our effort?** (What improvements will make the most difference?)

The Five-Pillar Diagnostic

Using the framework we've established throughout this book, you'll evaluate your organization's current state across each pillar. This isn't about achieving perfection; it's about understanding your unique starting point and building a roadmap that fits your situation.

Rate each statement below from 1-5 (1=Never/No, 5=Always/Yes):

Pillar 1 – Foundations Assessment:

1.1 Our governance documents (Articles, Bylaws) are current, accessible, and actually guide decision-making. ____

1.2 New board members can quickly understand how financial decisions get made in our organization. ____

1.3 We have written financial policies that staff and volunteers actually follow. ____

1.4 Our organizational structure creates appropriate checks and balances (no single person controls everything). ____

1.5 We have clear, documented procedures for key financial processes. ____

Pillar 1 Total: ____/25

Pillar 2 – Disbursements Assessment:

2.1 Every payment our organization makes has proper authorization and documentation. ____

2.2 We have clear spending limits that prevent unauthorized expenses while enabling efficient operations. ____

2.3 No single person can both approve and process payments without oversight. ____

2.4 Our expense reimbursement process is clear, fair, and consistently applied. ____

2.5 We properly classify workers as employees vs. contractors and handle payroll compliance correctly. ____

Pillar 2 Total: ____/25

Pillar 3 – Receipts Assessment:

3.1 Donations are handled securely from collection to deposit (two-person counting, prompt deposits). ____

3.2 We provide timely, compliant acknowledgments that meet IRS requirements and build donor relationships. ____

3.3 Restricted gifts are properly tracked and used only as donors intended. ____

3.4 Our electronic giving systems are secure, user-friendly, and properly integrated with our records. ____

3.5 We can quickly and accurately report on any donor's giving history and fund usage. ____

Pillar 3 Total: ____/25

Pillar 4 – Reporting Assessment:

4.1 We produce accurate financial reports within 20 days of month-end. ____

4.2 Our board receives financial reports they can understand and act upon. ____

4.3 Budget variances are identified, explained, and addressed promptly. ____

4.4 We maintain compliance with all required external reporting (Form 990, state registrations, etc.). ____

4.5 Financial information flows transparently to appropriate stakeholders when they need it. ____

Pillar 4 Total: ____/25

Pillar 5 – Implementation Assessment:

5.1 Our financial procedures are documented clearly enough to survive staff transitions. ____

5.2 Multiple people understand our key financial processes (no "heroic individual" dependency). ____

5.3 Staff receive adequate training on financial policies and their role in maintaining integrity. ____

5.4 We regularly review and update our financial systems as the organization grows. ____

5.5 Financial stewardship is part of our organizational culture, not just an administrative function. ____

Pillar 5 Total: ___/25

Overall Score: ___/125

Interpreting Your Results

Score Interpretation:

100-125 (Strong Foundation): Your financial systems are fundamentally sound. Focus on optimization and preparing for growth.

75-99 (Solid Base with Gaps): You have good systems with some vulnerabilities. Prioritize your lowest-scoring pillars while maintaining your strengths.

50-74 (Mixed Performance): Significant improvements needed in multiple areas. Use the prioritization matrix below to focus your efforts strategically.

25-49 (High Risk): Your financial systems pose serious risks to your mission. Immediate action required—consider professional assistance for implementation.

Below 25 (Crisis Mode): Stop everything and get help. Your current systems threaten organizational survival.

Pillar-by-Pillar Analysis:

Look at your individual pillar scores:

1. **Your strongest pillar (highest score):** This is your foundation to build from
2. **Your weakest pillar (lowest score):** This likely poses your greatest organizational risk
3. **Pillars scoring below 15:** These require immediate attention
4. **Pillars scoring 20+:** These can support improvements in weaker areas

The Prioritization Matrix

Not all improvements have the same impact. Use this matrix to identify where to focus your limited time and resources:

High Impact, Low Effort ("Quick Wins")

Do First: These improvements reduce significant risk while requiring minimal resources:
- Implementing two-person cash counting
- Creating basic approval limits for expenses
- Setting up automated donation acknowledgments
- Establishing monthly financial report deadlines
- Documenting critical procedures

High Impact, High Effort ("Major Projects")

Plan Carefully: These require significant investment but address fundamental vulnerabilities:
- Implementing comprehensive financial management software
- Developing complete policy manuals
- Restructuring governance for better oversight
- Creating sophisticated reporting systems
- Building redundancy in all critical processes

Low Impact, Low Effort ("Nice to Have")

Do When Convenient: These provide marginal benefits for minimal cost:
- Updating forms and templates
- Streamlining routine processes
- Improving filing systems
- Enhancing report formatting

Low Impact, High Effort ("Poor Investments")

Avoid Unless Mandated: These consume significant resources for minimal benefit:
- Over-engineering simple processes
- Implementing features few people will use
- Creating documentation that duplicates existing resources

Your Three-Step Action Plan

Based on your assessment results, here's how to get started immediately:

Monday Morning Step 1: Identify Your Biggest Risk

Look at your lowest-scoring pillar. What specific vulnerability could threaten your mission if left unaddressed? Write it down. This becomes your Priority #1.

Monday Morning Step 2: Find Your Easiest Win

From your Priority #1 pillar, identify one improvement you could implement this week with minimal resources. Maybe it's:
- Review your governing documents
- Creating a simple expense approval form
- Setting up two-person cash counting
- Implementing a monthly financial report deadline
- Documenting one critical procedure

Monday Morning Step 3: Get Leadership Buy-In

Schedule a conversation with your key leader (executive director, board chair, finance committee) to share your assessment results and proposed first step. Frame it this way: "I've identified a financial vulnerability that could impact our mission effectiveness.

Here's a simple first step that I would like to implement that will reduce our risk..."

Building Implementation Momentum

Remember: financial transformation is a marathon, not a sprint. Your assessment gives you the strategic roadmap, but lasting change happens through consistent progress over time.

Monthly Progress Reviews

Every month, ask three questions:
1. What financial risk did we reduce this month?
2. What system did we strengthen or improve?
3. What's our next highest-priority improvement?

Quarterly Reassessment

Every three months, retake portions of this assessment to track progress. You should see steady improvement in your lowest-scoring areas while maintaining strength in others.

Annual Strategic Review

Once a year, complete the full assessment to measure overall progress and adjust your improvement priorities based on organizational growth and changing circumstances.

Your Financial Foundation Awaits

You now have something most nonprofit leaders lack: a clear, objective picture of your organization's financial system health and a strategic framework for improvement.

The assessment reveals where you are. The prioritization matrix shows where to focus. The action plan gets you started immediately.

But here's what matters most: **taking the first step.**

Financial excellence isn't about perfection—it's about progress. It's about building systems worthy of your mission, one improvement at a time. It's about creating the financial foundation that enables your organization to thrive rather than merely survive.

The blueprint is in your hands. Your mission depends on what you build with it.

📌 BLUEPRINT NOTE

Your assessment results provide the strategic roadmap for strengthening your organization's financial system health. Focus on reducing your highest risks first while building momentum through quick wins. Remember: every improvement moves you closer to financial systems that unleash rather than constrain your mission impact.

☑ FINAL INSPECTION POINTS

☐ Have you completed the full five-pillar assessment honestly?

☐ Do you understand which pillar poses your greatest organizational risk?

☐ Have you identified at least one "quick win" you can implement immediately?

☐ Do you have leadership support for addressing your priority improvements?

☐ Are you committed to ongoing progress reviews rather than treating this as a one-time evaluation?

CONCLUSION

WE BEGAN THIS journey with a simple premise: the back office doesn't change lives, but it can make or break the work that does. After walking through the five pillars of financial health, exploring implementation strategies, and creating your assessment framework, that premise has evolved into something deeper and more compelling.

Financial systems aren't just administrative

necessities. They're strategic enablers of mission impact.

Think about where you were when you started reading this book. Maybe you were the executive director wondering if your organization's financial systems could support the growth you envisioned. Perhaps you were a board member concerned about financial accountability and oversight. Or maybe you were a staff member frustrated by financial processes that seemed to hinder rather than help your work.

Wherever you started, you now have something you didn't have before: a clear framework for understanding financial system health and a strategic approach to building systems that serve your mission.

What You've Gained

You've gained more than just knowledge about financial procedures. You've developed a leadership perspective on financial stewardship that connects every transaction to your organization's mission and values.

You understand the interconnected nature of financial health. The five pillars aren't separate systems—they're integrated components of a comprehensive framework. Strong foundations support effective disbursements. Proper receipt handling enables accurate reporting. Timely closing provides the information needed for strategic decisions. And implementation ties everything together into sustainable organizational capability.

You recognize the strategic value of financial excellence. Financial systems aren't overhead—they're infrastructure that enables mission achievement. When your financial house is in order, you can focus on programs rather than crisis management. When stakeholders trust your stewardship, they're more likely to support your work. When you can demonstrate impact through clear reporting, you build the credibility that attracts resources and partnerships.

You appreciate the leadership dimensions of financial management. Financial systems reflect organizational values and culture. The way you handle money communicates priorities, builds trust, and creates accountability. Leaders who understand this connection can use financial systems as tools for organizational development rather than just compliance requirements.

The Mission Connection

Throughout this book, we've emphasized that financial management in nonprofit organizations fundamentally differs from commercial enterprises. While businesses pursue profit, your organization pursues purpose. This difference should shape every aspect of how you approach financial systems.

Every financial decision reflects your values. When you implement dual controls for cash handling, you're not just preventing theft—you're demonstrating respect for donors' trust.

When you document procedures clearly, you're not just ensuring consistency—you're building organizational sustainability. When you provide timely financial reports, you're not just meeting compliance requirements—you're enabling informed decision-making.

Your financial statements tell the story of your mission in action. Behind every number is a program delivered, a life changed, a community served. When you ensure those numbers are accurate and timely, you're preserving the integrity of your mission story. When you present them clearly, you're helping stakeholders understand the impact of their investment.

Financial stewardship is a form of ministry. The way you handle resources entrusted to your care reflects your commitment to those who gave sacrificially and those you serve. Excellence in financial management isn't about perfection—it's about faithfulness to the trust placed in you.

The Implementation Imperative

Knowledge without action accomplishes nothing. The most brilliant financial framework provides no value if it remains theoretical. The test of everything you've learned in this book is whether you'll implement it in ways that strengthen your organization's mission effectiveness.

Implementation is a marathon, not a sprint. Financial transformation takes time, and attempting too much change too quickly often leads to resistance and abandonment. Use the phased approach outlined in Chapter 7 to build momentum through early wins while working toward larger objectives.

Culture change is as important as system change. People need to understand not just what to do but why it matters. Take time to connect financial procedures to mission impact. Address resistance with empathy and clear communication. Celebrate progress and learn from setbacks.

Leadership matters more than technique. The most sophisticated financial systems fail without appropriate leadership support. Leaders must model the behavior they expect, provide necessary resources, and create accountability for results. When leaders treat financial management as mission-critical rather than merely administrative, their teams will follow.

Your Next Steps

You now have the framework. You have the assessment tools. You have the implementation strategy. What you need next is the commitment to begin.

Start with your assessment. Use the five-pillar framework to evaluate your organization's current state honestly. Don't minimize problems or assume they'll resolve themselves. Create a clear picture of where you are today across all five areas.

Prioritize your improvements. Focus on changes that reduce significant risks while requiring reasonable effort to implement. Use the risk-effort matrix to identify your "quick wins" and build momentum for larger improvements.

Develop your plan. Create a phased implementation approach with realistic timelines, clear responsibilities, and regular evaluation points. Don't try to do everything at once—build sustainable change through consistent progress.

Secure leadership support. Connect your improvement plan to mission effectiveness and organizational sustainability. Help leaders understand how financial systems enable rather than constrain mission achievement.

Begin implementation. Start with your highest-priority, lowest-effort improvements. Document progress, celebrate successes, and learn from challenges. Use early wins to build support for more challenging improvements.

The Continuing Journey

This book represents the beginning of your journey toward financial excellence, not the end. As your organization grows and changes, your financial systems will need to evolve as well. The principles remain constant, but their application will adapt to new circumstances and challenges.

Stay connected to best practices in nonprofit financial management. The field continues evolving, and your knowledge needs to evolve with it. Attend conferences, participate in professional associations, and build relationships with other leaders facing similar challenges.

Build internal expertise rather than remaining dependent on external consultants. Invest in training for your financial staff, create succession plans for key roles, and develop internal capability that can support your organization's long-term needs.

Maintain perspective on the purpose of financial systems. They exist to serve your mission, not to become ends in themselves. When financial procedures start feeling like obstacles rather than enablers, step back and remember why they exist.

Continue learning from experience. Regular evaluation of your financial systems helps identify opportunities for improvement and ensures they continue meeting your organization's needs. What works well today may need modification tomorrow.

Your Financial Foundation

You now have the blueprint. The question is: what will you build?

Will you build systems that merely meet minimum requirements, or will you create infrastructure that enables extraordinary mission impact?

Will you implement changes that last only until the next transition, or will you build organizational capability that survives and thrives through leadership changes?

Will you view financial management as a necessary burden, or will you embrace it as a strategic tool for mission advancement?

The choice is yours. The framework is proven. The resources are available. The only question is your commitment to begin.

Your mission depends on it. Your stakeholders deserve it. Your community needs it.

The back office may not change lives directly, but with the right systems in place, it can absolutely enable the work that does.

Build well. Build wisely. Build for the long term.

Your financial foundation awaits.

The blueprint is in your hands. The rest is up to you.

APPENDIX

GLOSSARY OF KEY TERMS

A

Accounting Method: The systematic approach an organization uses to record financial transactions, typically cash basis, accrual basis, or modified cash basis.

Articles of Incorporation: The foundational legal document that establishes a nonprofit organization with the state. Most states refer to this foundational document as the *Articles of Incorporation*, there are three states that use a different term:

- Massachusetts – Articles of Organization
- New Hampshire – Articles of Agreement
- Connecticut – Certificate of Incorporation

B

Balance Sheet (Statement of Financial Position): A financial statement that shows an organization's assets, liabilities, and net assets at a specific point in time.

Board Governance: The system of rules, processes, and structures by which a nonprofit's board of directors guides the organization and ensures accountability to stakeholders.

Board-Designated Funds: Unrestricted assets that the board has set aside for specific purposes. Unlike donor-restricted funds, these designations can be changed or removed by board action.

Budget: A financial plan that projects expected revenues and expenses for a defined period, typically a fiscal year.

Budget Variance Report: A report that compares actual financial results with budgeted amounts, highlighting differences for analysis and explanation.

C

Capital Asset: A significant piece of property or equipment that has a useful life of more than one year. Examples include buildings, land, vehicles, and major equipment.

Capitalization Policy: A written policy that establishes the dollar threshold and criteria for determining when an expenditure should be recorded as a capital asset rather than an expense.

Cash Basis Accounting: A method of accounting that records revenues when cash is received and expenses when cash is paid out, regardless of when the obligation was incurred.

Chart of Accounts: A listing of all accounts used by an organization to record financial transactions in its general ledger.

Compilation: The lowest level of CPA service related to financial statements, where the accountant assembles financial information provided by management into standard financial statements without providing assurance.

Contribution: A voluntary, non-reciprocal transfer of cash or other assets to an organization, typically from a donor who receives no direct benefit in return.

D

Designated Funds: Funds set aside for specific purposes by the organization's governing board, rather than by external donors. These designations can be changed by board action.

Donor-Restricted Funds: Contributions with donor-imposed restrictions for specific purposes or time periods. These funds must be used according to the donor's specifications.

Dual Control: A financial control principle requiring two people to complete a sensitive task, such as counting cash or signing large checks, to reduce the risk of error or fraud.

E

EIN (Employer Identification Number): A nine-digit number assigned by the IRS to identify an organization for tax purposes, similar to a Social Security number for individuals.

External Audit: An independent review of an organization's financial statements and internal controls by qualified professionals not affiliated with the organization.

F

Fiduciary Responsibility: The legal and ethical obligation of leaders—such as board members, executive directors, and officers—to act in the best interests of the organization. Fiduciary responsibility includes the duties of care (making informed, prudent decisions), loyalty (placing the organization's interests above personal gain), and obedience (ensuring the organization follows its mission and complies with laws and governing documents). This responsibility extends to overseeing financial health, safeguarding assets, and maintaining transparency with stakeholders.

Financial Policies: Written guidelines that establish how an organization will handle financial transactions, make spending decisions, and maintain accountability.

Fiscal Year: A 12-month period used for calculating annual financial statements. May or may not coincide with the calendar year.

Fiscal Sponsorship: An arrangement where an established 501(c)(3) organization provides tax-exempt status and administrative support to a project or group that doesn't have its own tax-exempt status.

Five Pillars Framework: The comprehensive approach to nonprofit financial health designed to help nonprofit leaders evaluate and strengthen their operational and financial systems. The framework consists of five interconnected areas:

1. **Foundations** – Organizational structure, policies, and chart of accounts
2. **Disbursements** – Spending controls, payroll, and vendor management

3. **Receipts** – Income tracking, donor intent, and revenue integrity
4. **Reporting** – Month-end close, reconciliations, and board reporting
5. **Implementation** – Documentation, training, and long-term system resilience

Together, these pillars provide a comprehensive, strategic approach to building a backoffice that supports mission impact, transparency, and sustainability.

Form 990: The annual information return that most tax-exempt organizations must file with the IRS, providing information about the organization's mission, programs, and finances.

Fund Accounting: A method of accounting used by nonprofits that emphasizes accountability rather than profitability, tracking resources according to donor-imposed or board-designated restrictions.

G

GAAP (Generally Accepted Accounting Principles): The standardized set of guidelines, rules, and procedures used for financial reporting in the United States.

Grant: Funds given to an organization for a specific project or purpose, typically with reporting requirements and a defined time period.

I

Implementation Phase: The systematic process of putting financial policies and procedures into practice, including documentation, training, and ongoing monitoring.

In-Kind Contribution: A non-cash donation of goods, services, or other assets, such as donated supplies, professional services, or use of facilities.

Independent Contractor: A person or entity that provides services to an organization but is not treated as an employee for tax or legal purposes. The organization does not withhold taxes from payments to independent contractors.

Internal Controls: The procedures and policies designed to safeguard assets, ensure accurate financial reporting, promote operational efficiency, and encourage adherence to prescribed managerial policies.

L

Liabilities: Debts or obligations that represent amounts owed to others.

Liquidity: The ability of an organization to meet its short-term financial obligations as they come due.

M

Management Letter: A document provided by auditors after completing an audit, identifying internal control weaknesses and operational efficiency recommendations.

Mission Drift: The gradual shift away from an organization's core purpose and values, often occurring when financial pressures or opportunities pull focus from the original mission.

Modified Cash Basis Accounting: An accounting method that combines elements of cash basis and accrual basis accounting. Under modified cash basis, income and expenses are recorded when cash changes hands, but certain significant items—such as fixed assets, long-term liabilities, or payroll accruals—are tracked on an accrual basis for greater accuracy. Many nonprofits and small businesses use this method because it provides a clearer financial picture than pure cash basis without the complexity of full accrual accounting.

Month-End Closing: The systematic process of finalizing financial records at the end of each month, including reconciliations, adjustments, and report preparation.

N

Net Assets: The difference between an organization's total assets and total liabilities, representing the organization's equity. In nonprofits, net assets may be classified as with donor restrictions or without donor restrictions.

Non-Cash Donation: Contributions of goods or services rather than money, such as donated supplies, equipment, or professional services.

O

Operating Reserve: Funds set aside to provide financial stability and cover unexpected expenses or revenue shortfalls.

P

Program Expenses: Costs directly related to carrying out an organization's mission-related activities.

R

Restricted Funds: Assets that must be used for specific purposes as stipulated by donors.

Review: A financial service that provides limited assurance on an organization's financial statements, offering more scrutiny than a compilation but less than a full audit.

Risk-Effort Matrix: A prioritization tool that plots potential improvements based on risk reduction and implementation difficulty to identify "quick wins" and strategic investments.

S

Segregation of Duties: An internal control principle that prevents any single individual from controlling all phases of a transaction, reducing the risk of fraud or error.

Statement of Activities: A financial report that shows revenues, expenses, and changes in net assets over a specific period, telling the story of an organization's financial performance.

Stewardship: The careful and responsible management of resources entrusted to one's care, reflecting both competence and integrity in financial management.

T

Tax-Exempt Status: The IRS classification that generally exempts qualifying organizations from federal income tax and often allows donors to claim tax deductions for their contributions.

Taxpayer Identification Number (TIN): The TIN is a general term used for various identification numbers assigned by the IRS to taxpayers. EINs and SSNs are both TINs.

Temporarily Restricted Net Assets: Resources whose use is limited by donor-imposed stipulations that either expire with the passage of time or can be fulfilled by actions of the organization.

Two-Person Rule: A financial control requiring two unrelated individuals to count cash or handle sensitive financial tasks together, protecting both the organization and volunteers from theft or accusations.

U

Unrelated Business Income (UBI): Income from a trade or business regularly carried on by a tax-exempt organization that is not substantially related to the organization's exempt purpose.

Unrestricted Funds: Resources over which the board has discretionary control to use in achieving the organization's mission and objectives.

V

Variance Report: A financial analysis comparing actual results to budgeted amounts, highlighting differences that require explanation or corrective action.

W

W-2 Form: The tax form that reports an employee's annual wages and the taxes withheld from their paycheck.

W-9 Form: A request for a TIN and certification, typically completed by vendors or independent contractors before receiving payment.

Note: This glossary covers key terms referenced throughout this book and essential concepts for nonprofit financial leadership. While comprehensive for strategic purposes, it is not exhaustive of all accounting and financial terms you may encounter in nonprofit financial management.

ACKNOWLEDGEMENTS

WHILE THIS BOOK reflects both our voices and experiences, we each want to personally thank those who have shaped our journeys.

DELTON'S THANKS:

Thanks to the bride of my youth, **Pam**, for letting me dream big and pursue my passions without judgment or criticism (unless it's warranted!)

Thanks to **Adam** for joining me on this journey! You've supported me in so many ways. Thanks for believing in me.

Thanks to **Mike** at **BMWL** for seeing potential in me early on, then renewing your belief in me so many years later. Your encouraging words and actions speak volumes to my soul.

My time in Dallas profoundly impacted my understanding and involvement with nonprofits. My deepest thanks to **Bryan, Verne, Ann, Rodney, Rusty, Casey**, and others on the **PSK** team. You guys brought me into your family so many years ago during a season when kindness was both unexpected and welcomed. I look back on my time with you with fondness and gratitude. Thanks to **Bill** and the team at **Salmon Sims** for encouraging my development and renewing my passion and vigor while serving at my first paid position at a nonprofit. And special thanks to **Michael, Sarah, Josh, Laura, Jonathan**, and so many others who were patient with me as I found my nonprofit sea legs.

And I want to extend my sincere appreciation to **Thad** and **Ken** for your unwavering support. You deserve more credit than you'd ever be willing to accept.

And whatever I do, in word or deed, I do everything in the name of the Lord Jesus, giving thanks to God the Father through Him.

ADAM'S THANKS:

I, too, want to offer thanks to my family, friends, and clients, without whom my life and experiences would be incomplete and lacking!

Thanks to my best friend and wife, **Jennifer**, for all your support, encouragement, and perseverance with my self-inflicted schedule and workaholism!

Thanks to **Delton** for letting me tag along on this journey like a trail-ride at Santos.

Thanks to **Mike** and **Mike** and the **whole team at BMWL**, your level of professionalism and expertise is unparalleled! I have learned so much from you over the years.

Thanks to **Rob** for taking a chance on a 19-year-old kid with just an AA degree working his first real job in the world of accounting.

Thank to **Chap** and **Jef** for letting me talk you into the idea that construction is just the manufacturing of homes and becoming my first client.

Thanks to **all my clients** over the years who have given me the opportunity to learn from your industries from commercial construction to churches, from home building to horse breeding, from magazine distribution to online clubs, it has been a blessing to work with and learn from you!

A special thanks to **my church and nonprofit clients**, your mission to redeem broken spaces is inspiring. Care for the flock that God has entrusted to you. Watch over it willingly, not grudgingly—not for what you will get out of it, but because you are eager to serve God.

ABOUT THE AUTHORS

DELTON DE ARMAS is the founder of ICNU (Inspiring Churches to New Understanding), a consulting practice dedicated to helping churches, nonprofits, and small businesses establish clarity, structure, and sustainable financial systems to maximize their impact. With decades of experience in leadership, finance, and strategic development, Delton equips organizations with practical tools to move from vision to implementation—ensuring financial health, operational efficiency, and long-term sustainability.

Through ICNU, Delton works alongside pastors, executive leaders, and nonprofit directors to simplify complexity, improve financial stewardship, and develop effective systems that support—not stifle—their mission. His passion is empowering organizations to lead with confidence, steward their resources wisely, and sustain their impact for years to come.

Delton has undergraduate degrees in accounting and finance from the University of Central Florida, and earned a Master's in Biblical and Theological Studies from Dallas Theological Seminary. He blends faith, strategy, and stewardship to help leaders thrive in their calling.

He lives in Ocala, Florida, with his wife, Pam. When he's not working with organizations or writing, he enjoys cycling, songwriting, and deep, meaningful conversations about faith, resilience, and leadership.

To connect or learn more:
www.qavahministries.org
www.inspiringchurches.com
www.linkedin.com/in/delton-de-armas/

ADAM J. MOFFITT is a seasoned leader in church and nonprofit administration, operations, and financial management. With a career spanning over three decades, Adam has held top-level positions that have honed his expertise in guiding organizations toward 'operational excellence and fiscal responsibility.

He currently owns and manages Raeton, LLC, where he provides strategic consulting services that empower churches and nonprofits to strengthen their administrative frameworks and financial systems. His approach is rooted in a passion for excellence and a commitment to helping mission-driven organizations achieve sustainable success.

Adam received his Bachelor's of Arts degree in Business Administration from the University of South Florida with a concentration in Accounting & Finance. 150+ Hours for CPA Licensure in the State of Florida.

Beyond his consulting work, Adam and his wife, Jennifer, live in Winter Garden, Florida, and enjoy spending time with their married adult children, camping, and renovating properties.

To connect or learn more:
www.linkedin.com/in/adammoffitt/

OTHER WORKS BY DELTON DE ARMAS

Thrive: From the Inside Out

A redemptive memoir tracing Delton's journey through federal prison, personal transformation, and renewed purpose. This candid and hope-filled account explores the power of surrender, resilience, and service in seasons of suffering.

Thrive: A Study Guide

Designed for small groups, recovery programs, or personal growth, this companion resource helps readers walk through the lessons of *Thrive* with guided reflection, discussion questions, and real-life application.

Mo-Mentum Principles: Staying Balanced and Moving Forward

A story-driven business parable that demystifies cash flow for small business owners. Through a mentor's wisdom and a young entrepreneur's journey, readers learn how to lead with clarity and make better financial decisions.

The Thing That Matters: A Story about Being Different Together

A middle-grade chapter book inspired by the nine Enneagram types, this story follows a group of students tasked with planning a school event. Their clashing personalities seem like a recipe for chaos until they begin to recognize how their differences can actually work together. Perfect for classrooms, families, and small groups, this story invites readers to explore identity, empathy, and the power of belonging.

For more information or to explore bulk orders, visit:
www.inspiringchurches.com/books or
www.deltondearmas.com

To access tools and updates related to this framework, visit:

www.thebackofficeblueprint.com